EPPING

KING LEOPOLD

NAPIER

RANGES

Lennard River

Lennard River

Lennard River Station

Mount North Creek

RANGE

Windjana Gorge

Limalurru

Tunnel Creek (Cave of Bats)

OSCAR RANGE

Dingo Gap

Leopold Downs Station

Fitzroy River

Oscar Range Homestead

Brooking Gorge

Geikie Gorge

Brooking Springs

FITZROY CROSSING

Fossil Downs

Fitzroy River

Margaret River

MARK GREENWOOD
TERRY DENTON

JANDAMARRA

ALLEN&UNWIN
SYDNEY · MELBOURNE · AUCKLAND · LONDON

This book would not have been possible without the knowledge and guidance of Dillon Andrews, who took us to special sites connected with Jandamarra and taught us that this story is more than words — it is a treasured cultural inheritance. We respectfully acknowledge Bunuba custodianship of Jandamarra's story and are grateful for the consent of Bunuba Aboriginal Corporation. Special thanks to June Oscar for reviewing the manuscript and, with Patsy Bedford, for translating the phrase *Burrudi yatharra thirrili ngarra.*

Thanks also to Howard Pedersen, Keith Andrews, Selina Middleton, Emanuel James Brown, Dillon Andrews Jnr, Joshua 'Mossie' Brown, David and Eugenia Leslie, John Smoker, Jack Macale, Anita Heiss, Petrine McCrohan, Libby Letcher, Steve Hawke, Erica Wagner, Sarah Brenan, Ruth Grüner.

Burrudi yatharra thirrili ngarra
We are still here and strong

The boy had a Bunuba name,
given to him by his people.

But the boss at Lennard River
called him 'Pigeon', after the cheeky bird
that darted about the station.

For wages of flour and sugar,
Pigeon watched over sheep that grazed
on the black soil plains.

He listened and learned.
By the time he was fourteen,
Pigeon was the fastest shearer on the
station. He became a crack shot with a rifle
and could hit a target while standing in the
stirrups at full gallop.

While their sheep fattened on fertile pastures,
station owners fenced billabongs and sacred
Bunuba sites with post and rail.

But
Pigeon's people were
not willing to surrender
their country.

Bunuba hunters climbed down from the ranges.
Juicy meat was soon sizzling on cooking stones.

Before long, police were dispatched to arrest
the sheep thieves.

Scorching sun on iron blistered the prisoners' flesh
during the long march to Derby Jail.

Pigeon's loyalty to the station boss
ended when Bunuba elders took him on
a secret journey. He was taught the ancient
law of his people. He learned the stories of
the spirits that had sculpted the mountains
and rivers of his country.

'You will face many tests of courage,' warned his uncle, Ellemarra, 'before you become a Bunuba warrior.'

The long ritual of learning and understanding
was interrupted when troopers stormed Pigeon's
camp. He was accused of stealing a sheep, and
added to another chain of prisoners.

In Derby Jail the captives spent each night shackled
together. By day they laboured in stifling heat.
Some were sent away on steamships. They would
never see their country or their people again.

But Pigeon charmed the police with his cheeky grin and impressed them with his speed and agility.

In sports contests he was a nimble boxer and never beaten in a sprint.

When he tamed a wild stallion, Pigeon's talent was noted. He was recruited to care for police horses. In return he lived in the stables and was spared the overcrowded prison.

Two years came and went before
Pigeon was free to return to his ancestral land.
At the onset of the big wet he crossed flooded plains.

During Pigeon's time in jail, bellowing herds of cattle
had replaced sheep. The 'devil horns' were easy targets
for Bunuba hunters.

Station owners, outraged by the
constant spearing of their stock, prepared
to teach 'troublemakers' a brutal lesson.

Bunuba camps were attacked.
Suspected cattle killers were flogged or shot
in view of their women and children.

Hatred festered in Bunuba country.

Pigeon drifted from station to station.
He charmed women forbidden by his skin group
and broke sacred kinship law. Elders vowed
he would be punished.

At the police outpost, Limalurru,
Pigeon sought protection from Bunuba lawmen.
In return, he identified footprints for
Trooper Richardson and his tracker, Captain,
in their hunt for cattle spearers.

Pigeon led Captain across moonstruck plains.
They crept through bloodwoods without
snapping a twig or rustling a leaf. One by one,
wanted men were startled by the barrel
of a rifle pressed into their beards.

The capture of
Ellemarra crowned a
successful patrol.

Chained to a boab tree, sixteen accused
cattle thieves rattled their irons and demanded
to be released. 'Have you forgotten who you are?'
they said. 'We are your people.'

Ellemarra fixed his eyes on Pigeon. 'Free us,'
he whispered, 'so we can fight for our country.'

Pigeon tossed and turned,
trying to sleep. The voices of his uncles
and cousins haunted him. 'What should
I do?' he wondered. 'Stay loyal to my
friend Richardson? Or free my people
from their chains?'

At midnight Pigeon made his decision.

He crept towards the homestead.
Richardson was sleeping on flagstones
in the breezeway.

Pigeon lifted his rifle,
and fired.

Before the gunsmoke had cleared,
Pigeon was fumbling through the dead man's
pockets for keys to unlock the prisoners.

Once free, the mob began looting
the homestead. Pigeon buckled on a
cartridge belt. 'Trouble coming,' he warned.
'We'll need more guns.'

Smoke signals rallied warriors from near and far. They brought word of five hundred head of cattle and a wagon, loaded with supplies, rolling into Bunuba country.

Pigeon's gang waited in ambush at Windjana Gorge, alert for the stink of 'devil horns' carried on the wind.

Pigeon fired first.

A stockman fell
from his mare.

His chum spun around, but a bullet
ripped through his shoulder. Bunuba warriors
finished him off with spears.

The third drover, further back, heard
the crack of gunfire and galloped away
to raise the alarm.

The wagon contained a treasure of rifles and revolvers, and four thousand rounds of ammunition packed in grease. 'Enough to match the police,' said Pigeon, 'bullet for bullet.'

Pigeon and his gang were declared outlaws.

Police rode from Derby to dispense rough justice. At Windjana Gorge they dismounted and crept forward, shadowed by fortress walls.

Perched high up in the cliffs, Pigeon
and his men opened fire. Troopers dived
for cover behind fallen boulders.

All day, the sounds
of battle echoed off
the steep sides of
the gorge.

Ellemarra's back was ripped open by a deadly missile.

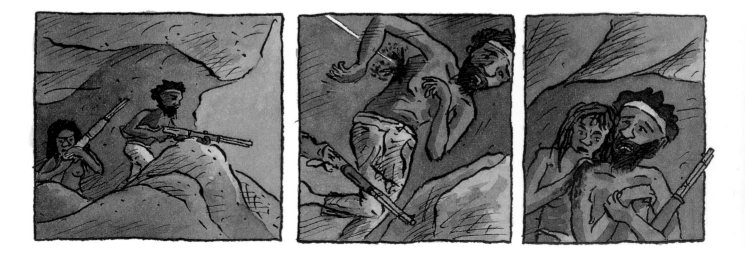

Bullets ricocheted off the roof of Pigeon's cave, shattering his shoulder, stripping flesh from his chest.

Women plastered his wounds with handfuls of dirt.

With victory impossible, Bunuba fighters scattered over the spires of the range.

Pigeon retreated into a crevice at the back of his cave.

He wormed his way deep into the mountain, testing the darkness with hands and feet.

Before nightfall, troopers rushed Pigeon's cave.

They found bloody handprints on the ledge, but no other trace of him.

Three hundred metres away, Pigeon emerged from the ranges.

Nursed by
Bunuba women,
he followed a creek,
then vanished
between tumbled
boulders that hid
the entrance to
a secret cave.

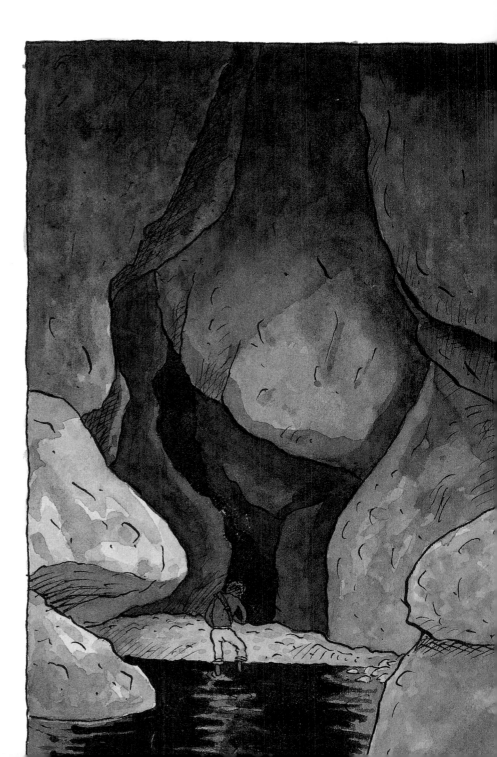

Pigeon waded through still, black water.
Eels slithered between his legs. On ledges near
the high-water mark, skulls and bones were
wrapped in bark shrouds. Above him, ghost bats
flapped their leathery wings.

Ahead, in the heart of the
cave, shafts of sunlight
speared in where the roof
had collapsed.

Weakened by his wounds,
Pigeon lay down beside
the living water.

Over the days and nights that followed,
he drifted in and out of consciousness.
In his dreams the ancestors comforted him
and sang away his pain. They rubbed him with
a magic stone to make him fearless and invisible.
They hid his spirit in the stone and
placed it in the water.

Outside, troopers scoured ravines
and criss-crossed the ranges, searching
for Pigeon and his gang.

Inside the cavern, their enemy was
hunched over a fire, feathers knotted
into his hair. His wounds had healed,
leaving bullets beneath his skin.

He emerged from the cave of bats
with the name given to him by his people.
He was Jandamarra,
a man with magic power – a Jalgangurru.
He could fly like a bird and appear
and disappear like a ghost.

Jandamarra haunted frontier homesteads. Sightings of him grew more frequent.

'He appeared on a ledge,' reported a trooper, 'and asked if I wanted to live or die — then blasted the hat from my head.'

News that the outlaw had risen from the dead prompted police to recruit a tracker with mystical powers. Micki could 'read' country for traces left by a fugitive.

He rode to the cave of bats to learn the secret of the man he would soon be hunting. From the living water he removed the magic stone and placed it on the ground. Jandamarra was no longer invisible to him.

Meanwhile, in the dead of night, Jandamarra
taunted police, hurling rocks onto the roof
as they tried to sleep, leaving his footprints
in flour sprinkled in the doorway.

Time and time again, with a patrol hot on
his heels, he vanished among anthills,
as if swallowed by the earth.

Cane grass was torched to drive him out,
but Jandamarra was never caught.

'He can fly like the bird that circles
the burning bush,' said Micki.

Jandamarra strung wire between trees to wrench his
pursuers from their horses. Bruised troopers swore
they'd show him no mercy.

The fugitive zigzagged across the plains,
bounding from boulder to boulder, sinking
into the crevices that riddled the ranges.

But the clip-clop of horse's hooves
was never far behind.

After weeks in the saddle, troopers
waited patiently for their most wanted
man to make a reckless mistake.

Micki now led the pursuit.

Jandamarra hauled himself up a jagged slope but pebbles dislodged by his feet gave away his position.

His pursuers fired,
reloaded and fired again.

Bullets peppered
Jandamarra's thighs.
He slipped from a ledge,
snapping his hip,
and squirmed away
in agony.

The outlaw
hid among
lilies in a soak
and waited
for danger
to pass.

He staggered
through Dingo
Gap, towards the
secret cave.

Another bullet
struck him in
the back.

Micki examined the tracks. "im tired fella,"
he muttered, and signalled to the troopers
to camp for the night.

Jandamarra was dreaming
of the living water.

**The illustrations for this book were done using
pencil, pen and (india) ink and watercolour on Arches paper.**

This project has been assisted by the Australian Government
through the Australia Council for the Arts, its arts funding and advisory body.

Australian Government   Australia Council for the Arts

First published in 2013
Copyright © Text, Mark Greenwood 2013,
with the permission of the Bunuba Aboriginal Corporation
Copyright © Illustrations, Terry Denton 2013

Allen & Unwin
83 Alexander Street
Crows Nest NSW 2065
Australia
Phone: (61 2) 8425 0100
Fax: (61 2) 9906 2218
Email: info@allenandunwin.com
Web: www.allenandunwin.com

A Cataloguing-in-Publication entry is available
from the National Library of Australia
www.trove.nla.gov.au

ISBN 978 1 74237 570 0

Teachers' notes available from www.allenandunwin.com

Cover and text design by Terry Denton and Ruth Grüner
Set in 16 pt blzee by Ruth Grüner
Colour reproduction by Splitting Image, Clayton, Victoria
This book was printed in November 2012 at Everbest Printing Co. Ltd
in 334 Huanshi Road South, Nansha, Guangdong, China

1 3 5 7 9 10 8 6 4 2

DERBY

Derby Jail

DERBY

BROOME

Fitzroy River

Scale: 1cm = 10km